Williamson Publishing

KNOTS TO KNOW 40
Hitches, Loops, Bends & Bindings

Emily Stetson

How-to Illustrations by
Marc Nadel

Illustrations by
Sarah Rakitin

Quick Starts for Kids!

WILLIAMSON PUBLISHING • CHARLOTTE, VERMONT

Library of Congress Cataloging-in-Publication Data

Stetson, Emily, 1957-
   40 knots to know : hitches, loops, bends & bindings / Emily Stetson; illustrations by Marc Nadel.
        p. cm. — (Quick starts for kids!)
   Includes index.
   Summary: Provides step-by-step instructions for tying five basic knots plus a variety of more complex ones, including joining knots, bindings, coils, hitches, lashings, and more.
   ISBN 1-885593-70-8 (pbk.)
    1. Knots and splices — Juvenile literature. [1. Knots and splices.] I. Nadel, Marc, ill. II. Title. III. Series.

   VM533.S74 2002
   623.88'82—dc21

                                                    2002016835

Me Tarzan!

Quick Starts for Kids!® series editor: **Susan Williamson**
Interior design and decorative illustrations: **Sarah Rakitin**
Interior technical illustrations: **Marc Nadel**
Cover design: **Marie Ferrante-Doyle**
Cover illustrations: **Michael Kline**
Cover photography: **Peter J. Coleman**
Printing: **Capital City Press**

Williamson Publishing Co.
P.O. Box 185
Charlotte, VT 05445
(800) 234-8791

Manufactured in the United States of America

10 9 8 7 6 5 4 3 2

◎ Dedication

In memory of my parents, Everett Halliday Stetson, Jr. and Edith Hurd Stetson, who showed me the ropes.

◎ Acknowledgments

With thanks to Susan Williamson, whose enthusiasm and editorial vision helped this kid-friendly knot guide take shape; to editors Vicky Congdon, Jean Silveira, and Dana Pierson, for their faithful attention to text and art details; to designer and illustrator Sarah Rakitin, for making the fun of tying knots shine through the pages; and to technical illustrator Marc Nadel, for his careful how-to renderings. Special thanks to Scout master, boatman, and knot enthusiast Winslow Ladue, for sharing his expertise and knot-tying insights throughout the process.

Contents

Foreword

Learning to tie knots was a rite of passage in my family. Once you knew how to tie a few secure knots, you were allowed to pack gear, put up the tent, and help out with the canoe and sailboat — coveted tasks among us four kids.

My parents were avid outdoorspeople, both having grown up in upstate New York. As a family, we canoed, hiked, and sailed near our home in rural western Pennsylvania and, when we got the chance, headed by car to the woods and lakes of the Adirondacks, to the mountains of New Hampshire and Vermont, and — on a few occasions — to the high peaks out West. One of my most frequent childhood memories is of my dad securing a canvas tarp to the roof rack of our bulging-at-the-seams station wagon — using all his skills as a former naval officer, no doubt. Those outings required plenty of knot know-how, and my mom, a top-notch canoeist and longtime camp counselor, was more than happy to share her knowledge. I learned to tie the versatile bowline; to use hitches to hang a food bag from a tree, pitch our old-fashioned canvas tent, and secure a boat; and — with my dad's help — to rig and coil the ropes on a sailboat. Boy, was I proud when I slept in my first makeshift tent, using a ground cloth tied over our canoe!

Knots were also a big deal at our house for everyday tasks, like stringing up the clothesline, fixing a broken trunk, hanging storage racks in the garage, and of course wrapping packages. Back then, all the out-of-town parcels were tied with twine, which we always had lots of, thanks to my mom. (We could have supplied the local post office with her on-hand stash!)

I still use those knots I first learned, plus a few more I've picked up since then. I've found that knots, once learned, never lose their usefulness in making everyday life a little easier and memorable adventures more doable.

Tie a few, and see for yourself what a knot can do!

Emily Stetson

The Quick Starts™ Guide to Tying Knots

If you've tied a shoelace, you're already a knot-tier. In fact, the best knots are very simple to tie (that's one of the characteristics of a good knot). And, because knots are related to one another, once you get the basics down, you quickly get to know the rest of the knot family.

So, where do you learn how to get the bind you want, when and where you need it? Right here! These knots — a mere sampling of the more than 4,000 knots humans have tied over the ages — cover the bases for just about any situation you might encounter. These are the knots people like you use every day, plus a few that are handy to know for not-so-ordinary days.

You'll find simple knots such as the RING HITCH (great for hanging a stopwatch from your belt loop), plus tried-and-trusted knots such as the FIGURE–EIGHT LOOP (good for rescues) and the TAUT–LINE HITCH (my favorite fix for sagging lines). I've also thrown in some fun yet practical knots that are just really cool to tie, like the MONKEY'S FIST.

NOW SAM WON'T RUN AWAY AGAIN!

Begin with the knots described in the *Quick Starts*™ "Fab Five" Knots, pages 10 to 18. If you intend to learn only a few knots, these five (with their variations) are definitely good ones to know. Or, if you have a specific task in mind, choose a knot from the typical situations on page 8 (and take a just-for-fun knot quiz while you're at it!). Turn the page for a quick rundown of the different types of knots you can tie.

Types of Knots

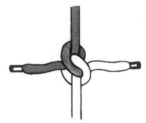

bends (pages 34 to 39): Used to *join together* two ropes to make a longer rope — handy to know when your shoelace breaks or you need a longer jump rope. Also known as *joining knots*.

bindings (pages 29 to 33): Used to *fasten together* the ends of cords or ropes to secure packages, bundles, and bandages. You also use a binding knot to tie a bow tie!

coils (pages 19 to 21): Used to *prepare a rope for storage.* You can also use coils to organize extension cords so that they don't tangle.

hitches (pages 46 to 54): These knots *tie a rope to something else* — a pole, post, or other object. Use them to secure a boat to a pier, a clothesline to a tree, or a leash to a railing.

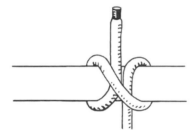

lashings (pages 55 to 60): *Combinations of knots* used to fasten poles (or ropes) together into structures. With them, you can make a fishing rod, a tepee, a bridge — even a raft!

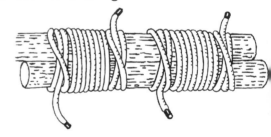

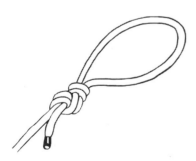

loops (pages 40 to 45): Used to *join a rope back to itself,* making a circle (or several circles). Some loops are *fixed* (the knot stays in one place), while others are *slipped* (the knot slides along the rope). Loop knots are great for all sorts of tasks, from rescues to hauling a sled or holding a water bottle.

shortenings (pages 22 to 23): These knots *take up the slack,* such as when you have an extension cord that's way too long.

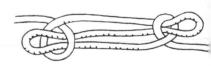

stopper knots (pages 24 to 28): Knots used to *prevent a rope from pulling free,* such as when you tie a knot at the end of a sewing thread, to *add weight at the end* (such as for a thrown line), or to *provide a grip* (such as on a tree-house rope ladder).

Knot Now!

To begin tying, you'll need a rope about 3 feet (1 m) long. Strictly speaking, *rope* means cordage of a certain width (at least ³/₈"/10 mm in diameter) that is twisted or braided together. Anything thinner is called cord, twine, yarn, string, or thread. But, don't panic, we aren't being overly picky on terms here. For easiest knot-tying practice, any cord about the thickness of a pencil will do, and for simplicity, we'll refer to it from here on as a rope or line. It can be made from natural fibers (like hemp or cotton) or from synthetic (man-made) fibers such as nylon, polyester, or polypropylene.

Put heavy tape around the ends of your rope to keep them from fraying. (You'll find some other ways to bind or fuse rope ends on pages 31 to 32, but this will do for starters.)

As you tie, keep in mind that there are two main parts to tying any knot: (1) *making the right tying steps in the correct order,* and (2) *tightening up the knot.*

Each tying step is clearly illustrated so you'll know just what to do. But before you really tighten the knot, *shape it* to get all the parts in place. Most knots need a little coaxing to get into position.

TAPE

Here are some of the tying terms you'll come across:

crossing: Any time ropes overlap each other.

loop: Crossings that form a circle in the rope. Can be **overhand** (the working end goes *over* the rope) or **underhand** (the working end goes *under* the rope).

standing part: The part of the rope that you aren't actually tying with (though you might tie over or under or around it). The **standing end** is the *inactive* end of the rope, or the end that is *already tied to something else* (such as to a boat or to your dog's collar).

working end: The active end of the rope that you're tying with.

bight: A line bent into a U-shape or semicircle.

draw-loop: A quick-release way to untie a knot, formed by leaving a bight in the working end.

tuck: Inserting the working end of the rope into another part of the knot.

turn: One complete wrap of the rope around itself or an object.

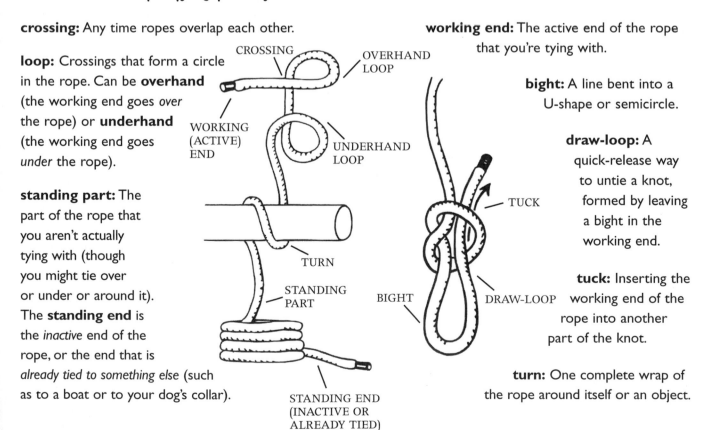

CROSSING · OVERHAND LOOP · WORKING (ACTIVE) END · UNDERHAND LOOP · TURN · STANDING PART · STANDING END (INACTIVE OR ALREADY TIED) · TUCK · BIGHT · DRAW-LOOP

The Know-It-All Knots Quiz!

One of the best places to start any new adventure, knot-tying included, is to "go to what you already know." Just for fun, glance down this list of 17 typical knot-tying tasks. Which *type* of knot would you use? (Stumped? See page 6 for a quick review of knot types.)

> what type of knot should you use, A. bend, B. bind, C. coil, D. hitch, E. lashing, F. loop, G. shortening or H. stopper, when you want to...

1. Make a tire swing?

2. Escape from a window on the second floor when all you have on hand are the sheets and bedspread on your bed?

3. Tighten the end of a drooping clothesline?

4. Tie the ends of a bandanna to make a sling?

5. Make a curtain cord hang down straight?

6. Tie a rope leash to your dog's collar?

7. Construct a bean tepee from poles or branches?

8. Make a bulky knot to hold beads on jewelry in place?

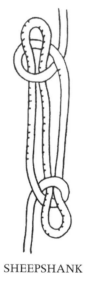

SHEEPSHANK

9. Fix your broken shoelace?

10. Hang a pendant around your neck?

11. Tie a dressy bow?

12. Make a homemade handle or a zipper pull?

13. Store loose string or cords?

14. Keep the end of a cotton rope from fraying?

15. Shorten the cord on your laptop computer (without unplugging the ends)?

16. Join two pieces of rope to make a sturdy line for towing?

17. Tie down gear to the roof of a car?

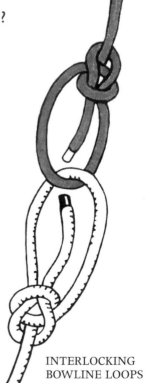

INTERLOCKING
BOWLINE LOOPS

Answers:

Missed some? Not to worry: You'll find every type of knot right here!

1. D. hitch. Use a knot that ties a rope to an object — such as a tire! Good choices would be the FISHERMAN'S BEND (also called an ANCHOR BEND), page 49 — yes, it really is a hitch! — or a CLOVE HITCH WITH TWO HALF HITCHES (page 48).

2. F. loop. You need a secure *fixed loop* to connect the bulky bedding. Interlocking BOWLINE LOOPS (page 13) work here.

3. D. hitch. The TAUT-LINE HITCH (page 50) is the best fix for adjusting the end of a sagging line.

4. B. binding. The SQUARE KNOT (pages 17 to 18) makes a good hold for a simple bind.

5. H. stopper. What you need is a heavy knot in the end of the cord that's easy to tie and looks good. Choose from either the HEAVING-LINE KNOT (pages 26 to 27) or the MONKEY'S FIST (pages 27 to 28).

DOUBLE SHEET BEND

6. D. hitch, or F. loop. For tying a rope to an object, such as the ring on a collar, or the collar itself, use TWO HALF HITCHES (page 16). Or, use a BOWLINE (page 12), tying the loop through the ring.

7. E. lashing. To bind three poles together into a structure, use a TRIPOD LASHING (page 58).

8. H. stopper. For this simple job, a simple knot like the DOUBLE OVERHAND (page 26) is all you need.

9. A. bend. Choose either a SHEET BEND or DOUBLE SHEET BEND (pages 14 to 15) or the simple OVERHAND BEND (pages 34 to 35) for this easy (but crucial!) task.

10. D. hitch. Use the RING HITCH (page 53) to hang an object from a looped chain.

11. B. binding. Easy — the BOW TIE (pages 30 to 31)!

12. G. shortening. What about a pull or homemade handle that looks like a braid but uses just one strand of rope? Try the BRAID KNOT (page 23).

CLOVE HITCH with TWO HALF HITCHES

13. C. coil. Keep it simple! Try the SIMPLE COIL (page 20).

14. H. stopper, or B. binding. Make do for the moment with a FIGURE-EIGHT (page 11) or OVERHAND KNOT (pages 24 to 25) or use WHIPPING (pages 31 to 32) for a permanent fix.

15. G. shortening. The SHEEPSHANK (page 22) works great for taking up the slack!

16. A. bend. A SHEET BEND (pages 14 to 15) will work for light jobs, while the CARRICK BEND (page 38) and the newer HUNTER'S BEND (page 39) are good knots to know for hefty hauling.

17. F. loop and D. hitches. Ask five people how they tie stuff down, and they'll give you five different answers. One favorite system (pages 44 to 45) uses the BOWLINE (pages 12 to 13), the FIGURE-EIGHT LOOP (pages 40 to 41), and TWO HALF HITCHES (page 16).

HEAVING-LINE KNOT

Of these 40 great knots, which are the most useful? Well, what knot you use depends on what you need it for. You'd never want to risk using a SQUARE KNOT in an emergency escape, for instance — that would be a sure disaster! You want the right knot for the job. So, the most important knots for you may depend on how you spend your free time and what chores you do.

The five knots (and a few of their variations) shown here — the FIGURE-EIGHT KNOT, the BOWLINE, the SHEET BEND, TWO HALF HITCHES, and the SQUARE KNOT — include five different types of uses: *stopping* a rope from pulling through; making a *secure loop; joining* two ropes together; *tying* a rope *to an object;* and making a *binding* knot for packages, bandages, or simple ties. If you're going to learn just a few knots, these are good ones to know.

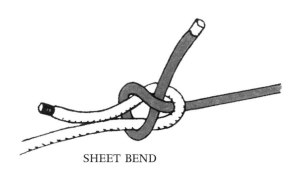

FIGURE-EIGHT KNOT

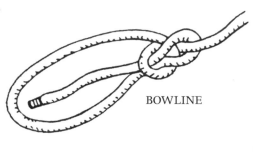

BOWLINE

SHEET BEND

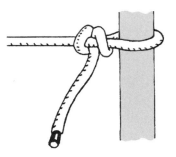

TWO HALF HITCHES

SQUARE KNOT

A Good Knot . . .

1. is easy to tie.

2. is easy to untie.

3. stays tied.

Of course, a knot is only as good as the speed and ease with which you can tie it, too. You never know when you'll need to tie a knot in the dark (or underwater, even). With a little practice, you'll be able to tie these knots with your eyes closed — as simple as tying your shoes in the dark!

Figure-Eight Knot

🌀 **Description:** A stopper knot, tied in the end of a rope to keep it from slipping through or to make it easier to hang onto.

🌀 **Uses:** The FIGURE-EIGHT KNOT is so easy to tie *and* untie that it's a favorite of rope users. For starters, it's used at the ends of the *sheets* (ropes) on a sailboat, to keep them from slipping through a chock or pulley. The FIGURE-EIGHT is also used on a lasso — *Yee-haw!* You can use it to knot the end of a shoelace or a frayed rope, to make grips on a tree-house climbing rope, or to stop a rope handle from pulling through the front of a sled. Plus, the FIGURE-EIGHT can be easily tied in a loop (pages 40 to 41), a bend, a hitch, or a coil. Useful? You bet!

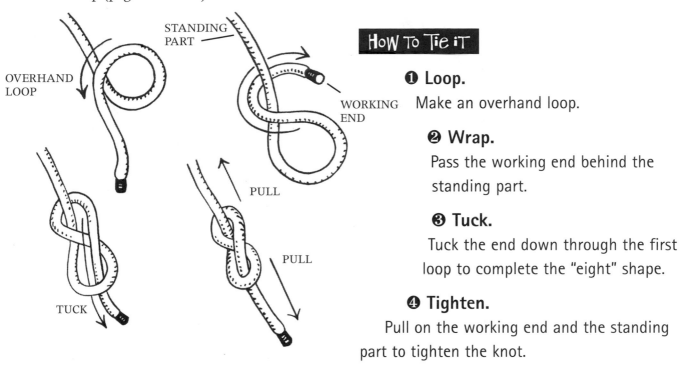

OVERHAND LOOP · STANDING PART · WORKING END · PULL · TUCK · PULL

How to Tie it

❶ Loop.
Make an overhand loop.

❷ Wrap.
Pass the working end behind the standing part.

❸ Tuck.
Tuck the end down through the first loop to complete the "eight" shape.

❹ Tighten.
Pull on the working end and the standing part to tighten the knot.

🖐 Quick Starts™
Tying Tips

Tie it another way. OK, now that you've got that technique down, try this:

1. Form a bight.

2. Give it two twists.

BIGHT

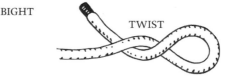
TWIST

3. Tuck and tighten as in steps 3 and 4 above.

What do you have? It's the same knot, just made in a different way. That's one of the cool things about tying knots — there's often more than one way to end up with the same knot. Which method is easier to tie? You choose!

Bowline

"You may call me "your Majesty."

Description: The BOWLINE (pronounced BOH-linn) forms a loop that won't slip, come loose, or jam, and it is easy to tie and untie even when wet.

Uses: This "king of knots" is used in camping, sailing, mountaineering, rescues — you name it! Use it to make a sturdy loop to place over a cleat or post, or tie it around someone's waist in a trusty rescue loop. You can also use a BOWLINE to attach a rope to something else — to the *grommet* (a reinforced ring) on a tarp or sail, to a mooring ring, or to a car roof rack (page 44), for instance

HOW TO TIE IT

❶ Loop.
Make an overhand loop.

❷ Wrap and tuck.
Bring the rope's working end up through the loop, behind the standing part, and back down into the loop.

❸ Tighten.
Pull up on the standing part while you also pull down on the loop and working end. Make sure there's plenty of rope tucked down through.

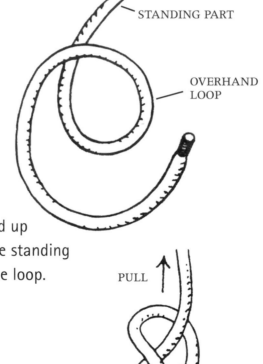

STANDING PART

OVERHAND LOOP

BEHIND

BACK DOWN

WORKING END

UP

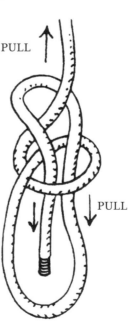

PULL

PULL

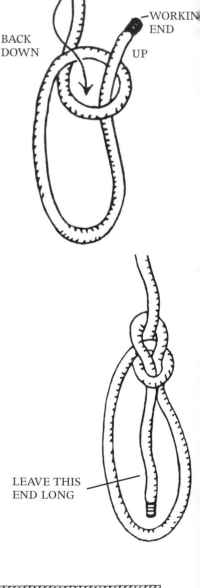

LEAVE THIS END LONG

Quick Starts™
Tying Tips

Follow the bunny. Want an easy way to remember this knot after you make the overhand loop? Think of a rabbit, coming out of its hole (the overhand loop), going behind the tree, and then popping down in front again. You'll get it right every time!

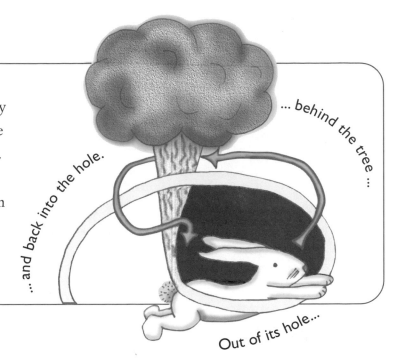

...and back into the hole.

...behind the tree ...

Out of its hole...

More Knots to Know

• **Add a stopper.** For added security, finish the end of the BOWLINE with a stopper knot, such as the FIGURE-EIGHT (page 11) or the DOUBLE OVERHAND (page 26).

• **Interlocking bowlines** can be used to join two different-sized ropes or to make an emergency escape line using bulky material (such as the sheets from your bed). Make the first BOWLINE in one rope. As you make another BOWLINE in the second rope, loop it through the first BOWLINE.

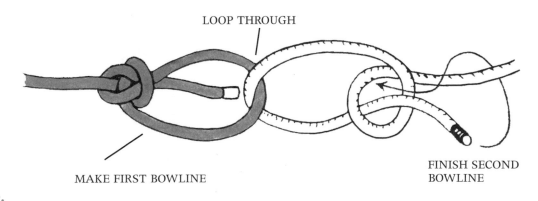

LOOP THROUGH

MAKE FIRST BOWLINE

FINISH SECOND
BOWLINE

Sheet Bend

◎ **Description:** This knot joins the ends of two ropes together, and — unlike most knots — it's not terribly picky about rope thicknesses: It's one of the few bends you can use to join two different-sized ropes that will be kept *taut* (tight).

◎ **Uses:** Good for mending a clothesline or making a longer line with two different ropes, tying yarn together in weaving or knitting, fixing a broken shoelace, or joining two ropes to make a light-use towrope. (For tough jobs, try the GRAPEVINE KNOT, HUNTER'S BEND, or CARRICK BEND, pages 37 to 39.)

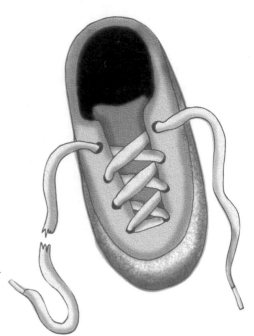

i BET a SHEET BEND WOULD FIX US UP!

HOW To Tie iT

❶ Bend and thread.
Form a bight in the thicker rope. Insert the working end of the thinner rope up through.

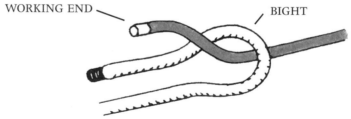

WORKING END   BIGHT

❷ Wrap and tuck.
Wrap the working end of the thinner rope around the thicker rope and back under itself. (Don't forget that tuck — it's very important! When tied correctly, both of the short ends are on the same side of the knot as shown.)

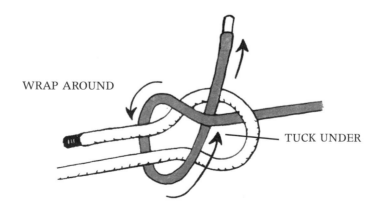

WRAP AROUND   TUCK UNDER

❸ Tighten.

Pull the standing parts of both ropes to tighten.

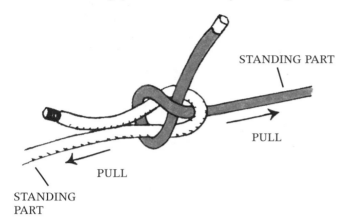

STANDING PART

PULL

PULL

STANDING PART

**Quick Starts™
Tying Tips**

Tight is right. Once the SHEET BEND is made, it needs to stay tight in order to hold. If you're looking for extra security — especially important if you're using slippery or synthetic-fiber ropes — try the doubled version (see below) or even a tripled SHEET BEND.

Knot Notes

What's in a name? The SHEET BEND has a U-shaped bend (the bight) that's made in the thicker rope; a *bend* is also another name for a knot that joins two rope ends. Any ideas for the *sheet*? Nope, it doesn't refer to what you sleep under. It's the *nautical* (sailing) name for the ropes that control the corners of the sails on a sailboat, where a SHEET BEND can be mighty useful!

⟶ More Knots to Know ⟵

Double sheet bend. Follow the directions for the SHEET BEND, but make two wraps with the thinner rope to help hold the bight in the larger rope.

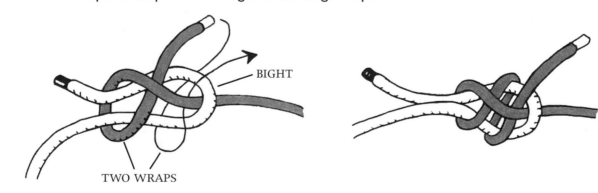

BIGHT

TWO WRAPS

Two Half Hitches

🌀 **Description:** This knot is just what its name suggests: *two* HALF HITCHES, tied one right after the other, snugged up tight. It's a handy knot that stays secure even when tied around a square shape, such as a railing, or when shaken a lot.

🌀 **Uses:** TWO HALF HITCHES attach a rope to a post, a grommet, a mooring ring, or to the rail of your porch. Use it on its own or as a "helper" with other knots, such as the CLOVE HITCH (page 48) or SQUARE KNOT (page 18), to make them more secure. Once you know how to tie TWO HALF HITCHES, it's a cinch to tie other hitches! See pages 48 and 49 for more variations.

ONE HALF HITCH

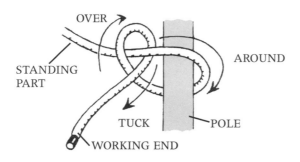

OVER

STANDING PART

AROUND

TUCK — POLE

WORKING END

HOW TO TIE IT

❶ **Wrap and tuck.**
Pass the working end of the rope around the pole or post, then over and under the standing part, tucking through the loop you just made. Congratulations! You've just tied one HALF HITCH.

❷ **Wrap and tuck again.**
Make a second HALF HITCH around the standing part.

❸ **Tighten.**
Push the HALF HITCHES together, and pu[ll] the working end to tighten the knot.

MAKE A SECOND HALF HITCH

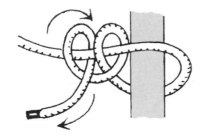

PUSH

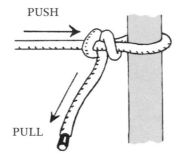

PULL

Quick Starts™
Tying Tips

Slipped two half hitches. The only downside to TWO HALF HITCHES is that this knot can be a bit tricky to untie when it's pulled really tight. For quick releases, leave a draw-loop when you make the second HALF HITCH. To untie, pull on the free end, and the loop will slip open, leaving a simple-to-undo HALF HITCH.

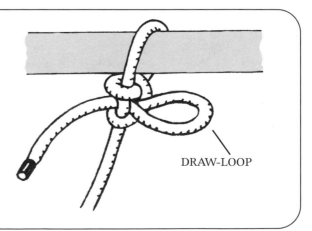

DRAW-LOOP

40 KNOTS TO KNOW

Square Knot

🌀 **Description:** You may know this binding knot already. It's that familiar "right over left, left over right" knot. It's a light-duty knot used to fasten two ends of rope.

🌀 **Uses:** Good for simple jobs like tying ribbon on packages, fastening the ends of a sling, or holding a rolled-up sleeping bag together. (Sailors traditionally used it to "reef" or furl their lowered sails, so it's also known as the REEF KNOT.) The bowed version (pages 29 to 30) holds the laces of your shoes in place!

HOW TO TiE iT

❶ Position.

Hold one end of the rope in each hand. (For easy viewing, we've shaded the right-hand rope.)

❷ Cross over and under.

Cross the right-hand rope over and under the left-hand rope and back up. (It's the "right over left.")

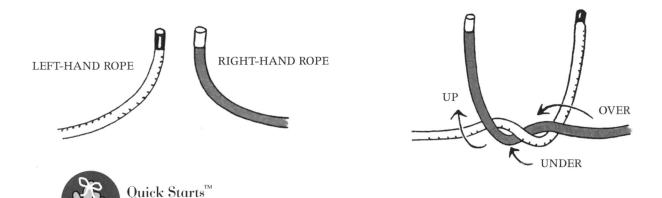

LEFT-HAND ROPE   RIGHT-HAND ROPE

UP   OVER   UNDER

![Quick Starts™ Tying Tips]

Quick Starts™
Tying Tips

• **Capsized!** Though the square knot is very useful for quickly tying (and untying) the ends of string, small cords, and ropes, it is *not* the knot you want to use to tie a boat to a dock or to link two ropes together to climb up to a tree house. That's because the square knot comes undone, or *capsizes,* when jiggled or bumped, especially when tied in a thick rope or in slippery nylon ropes. Here's the rule: *Never use the square knot to join ropes that move or might carry a load* — like you!

• **Capsizing a square knot.** Pull on one end in the opposite direction from which it came. Then, slide the end out to pull the whole knot apart.

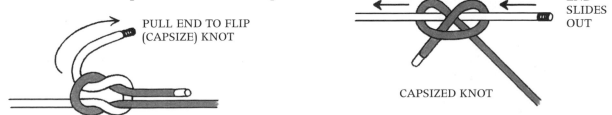

PULL END TO FLIP (CAPSIZE) KNOT

END SLIDES OUT

CAPSIZED KNOT

❸ **Cross over and under again.** Using the *same rope end that you started with* (now in your left hand), cross over and under again. (This is the "left over right" part.)

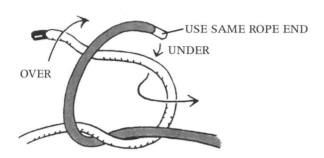

❹ **Tighten.**

Pull the ropes tight. You'll see a square (a diamond, actually) in the middle of the knot.

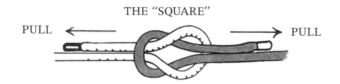

Quick Starts™
Tying Tips

No grannies, please! On a proper SQUARE KNOT, both ends come out on the same side of the loop, making a flat knot. The knot can be tied "right over left, left over right" or "left over right, right over left" — either way works. If you forget the rule and don't reverse the tying, you'll end up with the much less reliable GRANNY KNOT, which can jam or slip.

Granny knot

⌇ **More Knots to Know** ⌇

• **Surgeon's knot.** Pass the rope end around an extra time as you make each crossing (SQUARE KNOT, page 17, step 2 and above, step 3), and you'll have this tidy knot, also known as the SUTURE KNOT. It's best when used with fine cord, such as in making jewelry with monofilament line. The first extra wrap helps hold the rope in place — a good knot to remember when you're tying a package and there's no one to lend a finger to hold it tight! The second extra wrap is optional.

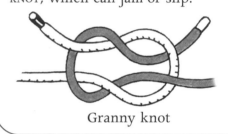

SECOND EXTRA WRAP (OPTIONAL)

FIRST EXTRA WRAP

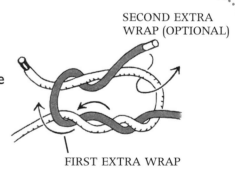

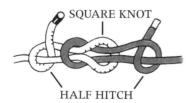

SQUARE KNOT

HALF HITCH

• **Add a hitch.** To make the SQUARE KNOT more secure, add a HALF HITCH or even TWO HALF HITCHES (page 16) to each end.

Coils & Shortenings

The basics of rope care are easy: Keep ropes clean, dry, and untangled. The clean and dry part is up to you, but coils and shortenings can help you make sure ropes and other cords stay tangle-free. They'll help you organize phone and computer cords, jump ropes, extension cords, hoses, string or yarn, even embroidery floss.

Three Easy Coils

Description: Wraps that keep lines untangled, so they're easy to unwind and ready to use.

Uses: Great for storing extra ropes, extension cords, jump ropes, clotheslines, water-skiing towropes, boat lines.

Quick Starts™
Tying Tips

Go with the flow. To make a coil, place the rope, with the end hanging down, over your palm. With your other hand, guide the rope back up to your hand, leaving a long loop (some people like to make the loop around their elbow). That makes your first coil. To help eliminate kinks, roll the rope a half turn as you lay it in your hand. Always coil with the lay of the rope — the way it naturally wants to wind. For most ropes, that means coiling clockwise. Going against the natural winding may cause it to jam and tangle.

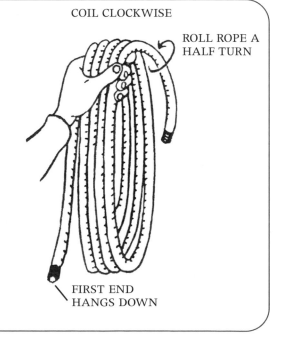

COIL CLOCKWISE

ROLL ROPE A HALF TURN

FIRST END HANGS DOWN

Simple Coil

🌀 **Uses:** Good for storing large or small ropes and cords.

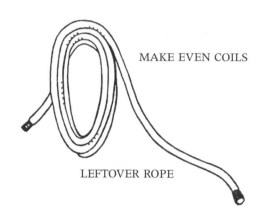

MAKE EVEN COILS

LEFTOVER ROPE

HOW TO TIE IT

❶ Coil.
Wind the rope in even coils until you have about a loop's length left.

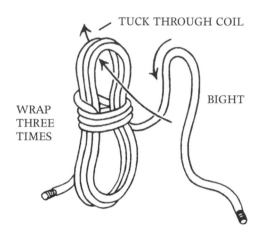

TUCK THROUGH COIL

WRAP THREE TIMES

BIGHT

❷ Wrap and tuck.
Wrap the remaining rope around the middle of the coils three or four times. Make a bight in the remaining rope and tuck it under and through the top of the coil.

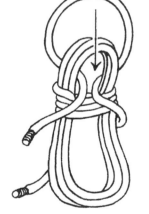

BEND BIGHT DOWN OVER COIL

❸ Bend back.
Open up the top of the bight and bend it back over the coil.

PULL END

❹ Tighten.
Pull up on the free end to tighten the coil evenly. *Voilà!* Your rope is ready for storage!

Hanging Coil

◎ **Uses:** A good way to hang ropes for easy storage and reuse.

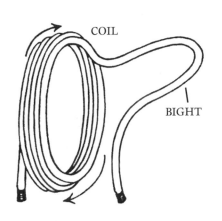

COIL

BIGHT

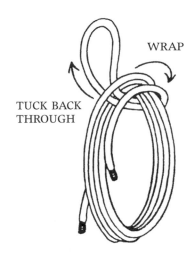

WRAP

TUCK BACK
THROUGH

HOW TO TIE IT

❶ Coil and make a bight.
Coil the cord. Make a bight with the free end.

❷ Wrap and tuck.
Wrap the bight around the top of the coil, then tuck it back through itself.

❸ Wrap and tuck again.
Make a second wrap around the coil and tuck the loop through.

❹ Hang.
Hang from the loop.

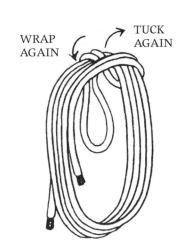

WRAP
AGAIN

TUCK
AGAIN

HANG FROM LOOP

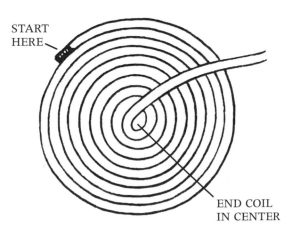

START
HERE

END COIL
IN CENTER

Flat Coil

◎ **Uses:** Good for neatly organizing the excess length in a line that's in use, such as on a dock.

HOW TO TIE IT

❶ Lay the outer circle first.

❷ Coil in toward the center in a clockwise direction.

Simple Shortenings

Sheepshank

What do you do when a rope's too long and you can't coil the ends? Give it the sheepshank treatment!

◎ **Description:** A temporary knot for taking up the slack in fastened lines, when you can't use the ends.

◎ **Uses:** Great for too-long phone cords, computer cords, extension cords, and ropes.

HOW TO TIE IT

❶ Make two bights.
Take up the slack by creating two bights.

❷ Loop.
Make an underhand loop in each end. Slip one loop over each side of the doubled rope as shown.

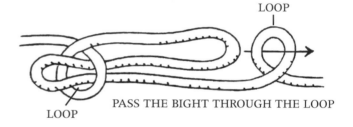

PASS THE BIGHT THROUGH THE LOOP

❸ Tighten.
Pull the knot snug by pulling on the ends.

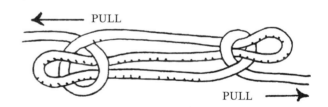

PULL

PULL

Quick Starts™
Tying Tips

Loop it again. The SHEEPSHANK will hold the slack on a rope, *but only as long as there's a pull on the rope.* If the rope or cord is still too slack, the loops at the ends will tend to pull out. To make the knot more permanent, add a second underhand loop to each end.

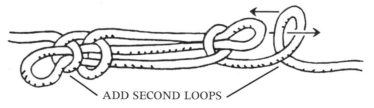

ADD SECOND LOOPS

Braid Knot

🌀 **Description:** A simple braid made from a single strand of rope!

🌀 **Uses:** To shorten a long length of line, to make a decorative zipper pull, or to make a homemade luggage handle.

Squeak, Squeak, Squeak.

HOW TO TIE IT

❶ Position.

Arrange the rope as shown.

❷ Braid.

Bring alternate outer strands across the middle strand, just as you would to make a normal braid. Repeat the crossovers, unbraiding the section *below* your fingers as you go.

❸ Tuck.

Make a locking tuck in the end loop.

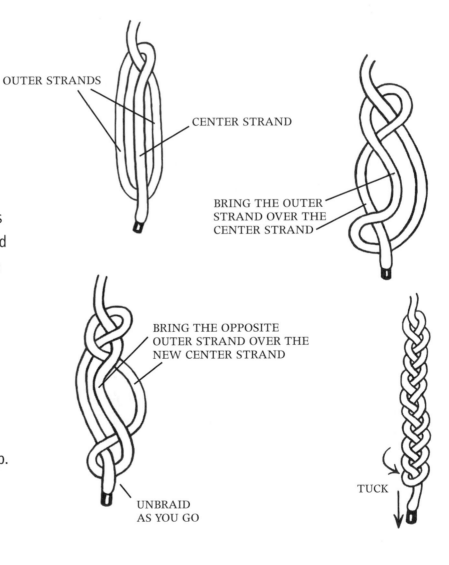

OUTER STRANDS

CENTER STRAND

BRING THE OUTER STRAND OVER THE CENTER STRAND

BRING THE OPPOSITE OUTER STRAND OVER THE NEW CENTER STRAND

UNBRAID AS YOU GO

TUCK

Stopper & End Knots

Me Tarzan!

S topper knots prevent rope, thread, or string from slipping or pulling through a small opening. Some can be tied anywhere on the rope, but they're most often tied at the end (that's why they're also known as *end knots*). These knots come in handy when you want to secure a rope end to a swing or sled, make beaded jewelry, or string a musical instrument. You can also use these bumplike knots to make a rope ladder or Tarzan swing, or for grips on a tug-of-war rope. Of the stoppers shown here, the OVERHAND KNOT is the smallest, with the popular easy-to-tie (and untie!) FIGURE-EIGHT KNOT (page 11) being just a bit bigger, the HEAVING-LINE KNOT larger still, and the decorative MONKEY'S FIST the largest.

Overhand Knot

You've used this knot loads of times. It's the basis for many other knots.

◎ **Description:** Stops a line from slipping or pulling through a hole. Difficult to untie, especially when wet.

◎ **Uses:** For knotting thread ends, stringing a musical instrument, or making a quick fix in the end of a rope to keep it from unraveling. An overhand knot that slips (page 43) makes a good knot for the end of a yo-yo string.

How To Tie iT

❶ **Loop.**
Make an overhand loop (over the standing part of the rope).

❷ **Tuck.**
Cross under, tucking the end up through the loop.

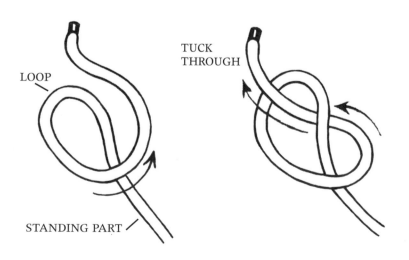

LOOP

TUCK THROUGH

STANDING PART

❸ Tighten.

Pull the knot snug.

PULL

Quick Starts™
Tying Tips

Man overboard! Here's a neat trick to get evenly spaced overhand knots on a rope: Hold the end of the rope in your left hand, palm up. Make a loop in the rope with your right hand and pass it to your left hand as shown. Repeat the loop-making step until you're at the end of the rope. Then pass the first end through all the loops. As you pull the rope through, you'll get a chain of overhand knots — perfect for a Tarzan rope!

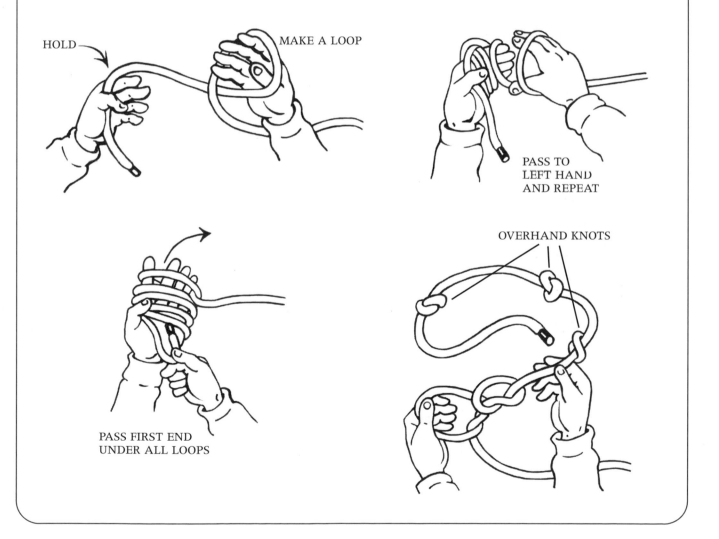

HOLD

MAKE A LOOP

PASS TO LEFT HAND AND REPEAT

PASS FIRST END UNDER ALL LOOPS

OVERHAND KNOTS

Double overhand. Used to make a bulkier knot. Twist and pull the ends as you tighten the knot.

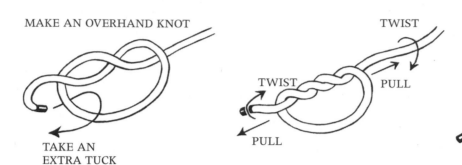

MAKE AN OVERHAND KNOT

TAKE AN
EXTRA TUCK

TWIST

PULL

TWIST

PULL

Heave-Ho!

Heaving-Line Knot

◎ **Description:** A special kind of stopper knot that adds weight to a rope. Strong and easy to untie.

◎ **Uses:** For ropes that will be *heaved* (thrown) or hung, like an emergency line or a pull cord for blinds or curtains. Sailors use it to help toss out lines, but you can also use this knot on a rope tied as a belt or as a bulky stopper knot.

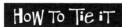

HOW TO TIE IT

❶ **Loop.**

Make a long overhand loop, leaving plenty of extra line at the working end.

❷ **Wrap.**

Make repeated turns around the loop.

WORKING
END

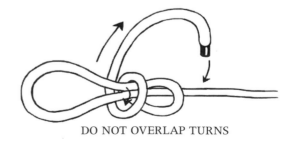

DO NOT OVERLAP TURNS

❸ Tuck.

Pass the working end through the overhand loop.

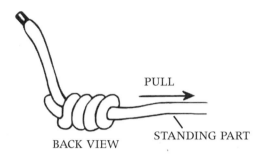

TUCK

WORKING END

❹ Tighten.

Pull on the standing part to snug up the knot.

PULL

BACK VIEW STANDING PART

Quick Starts™ Tying Tips

No overlap. When you make the repeated turns, be sure not to cross them. You want the turns to be side by side, not on top of one another. The more turns you add, the heavier the knot will be.

CHECK ME OUT!

Monkey's Fist

Want a challenge? This cool-looking end knot is used mainly for decoration, but it can also be used as a make-it-yourself button!

 Description: A knot that makes a ball in the end of a rope.

 Uses: For handmade buttons, decorative curtain or blind pulls, belt ends, fancy heaving lines, even kitty toys.

HOW TO TIE IT

❶ Wrap.

Coil the rope three times around your hand, leaving a long end.

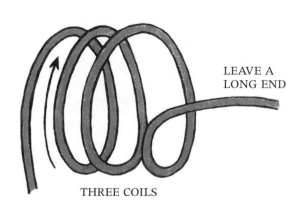

LEAVE A LONG END

THREE COILS

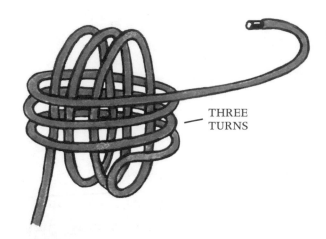

THREE
TURNS

❷ Wrap again.

Make three horizontal turns outside
the middle of the first three turns.

❸ Wrap a final time.

Make three more turns, passing
inside the first set of turns and
outside the second set.

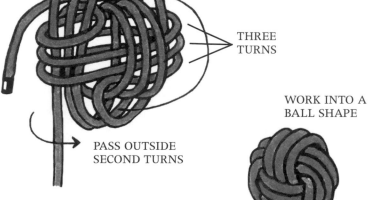

PASS INSIDE
FIRST TURNS

THREE
TURNS

PASS OUTSIDE
SECOND TURNS

WORK INTO A
BALL SHAPE

❹ Tighten.

Work the knot into a ball shape, and
tighten. If you want the end to be tied
back, WHIP it (pages 31 to 32) to the
standing part of the rope.

STANDING
PART

Quick Starts™
Tying Tips

Yarn trick. To get a perfectly round knot, put a tiny ball of yarn or fabric
batting inside the center of the MONKEY'S FIST before you tighten the knot.
(Please don't use any type of hard or heavy object in the core!)

In a Bind: Binding Knots

B inding knots are the unsung heroes of everyday life. They are used to wrap packages, tie shoes, secure bandages, cinch up sacks, make bow ties — even close a wound! They're usually used to join the ends of a rope around an object (a sling around your arm, a bow around your neck, or a tie around the open end of a bag, for instance). A binding knot rests against or "bears upon" the object it holds, keeping everything bound up just right. The SQUARE KNOT (pages 17 to 18) is the most well-known binding knot; here, you'll find two of the SQUARE KNOT's variations, along with the ever-tight CONSTRICTOR KNOT and a handy WHIPPING knot.

If getting in a bind is what you're after, you're looking in the right place!

Square Bow

◎ **Description:** This knot, also called the DOUBLE REEF BOW, is tied like a typical SQUARE KNOT (pages 17 to 18), except that you tie the second crossing with two draw-loops.

◎ **Uses:** To tie your shoes, make a bow on a package, or tie a bow for a wreath or decoration. (For a slightly fancier variation, try the BOW TIE, pages 30 to 31.)

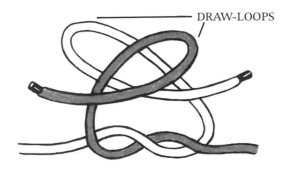

DRAW-LOOPS

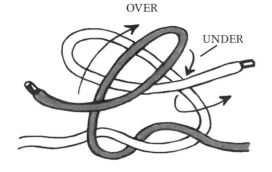

OVER

UNDER

HOW TO TIE IT

❶ **Cross over and under.**
Cross one end over and then under (right over left) the other end, just as you would for the first part of making a SQUARE KNOT (page 17, step 2). Pull snug.

❷ **Make two draw-loops.**
Holding the two ends you just crossed, make a bight in each end. These are your draw-loops.

❸ **Cross over and under again.**
Cross the loops over and under again, from the opposite side (left over right).

❹ Tighten.
Pull loops to tighten.

PULL ← PULL →

Bow Tie

◉ **Description:** The "tricky" BOW TIE is like the SQUARE BOW (page 29), but tied in a slightly different way.

◉ **Uses:** For making a neat bow with ribbon on packages, and in flat material, for a fancy bow tie around your neck.

School Picture Today

NEXT!

How To Tie iT

❶ Tie "left over right" and make a bight.
Wrap the rope around a parcel to practice. Take the left-hand end over and under. Make a bight in the other end (this will become your first draw-loop).

❷ Up and over.
This is where it gets tricky. Bring the top strand down and make a second draw-loop.

❸ Tuck.
Tuck the second draw-loop behind the first draw-loop and back up through.

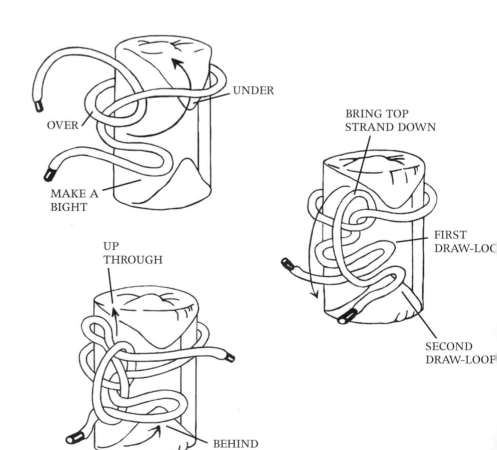

OVER

UNDER

MAKE A BIGHT

BRING TOP STRAND DOWN

FIRST DRAW-LOOP

SECOND DRAW-LOOP

UP THROUGH

BEHIND

❹ Tighten.

Pull the loops tight to finish.

Whipping

Ever heard the expression "I'm at the end of my rope!"? Usually people say it when they're losing their patience or are tired. Or, someone might say that he is becoming "unraveled" or "frayed." Well, that's just what a rope does when it gets worn out, too.

To help out a frayed rope, or to keep a rope from unraveling in the first place, you need to give it a good whipping (that's where the comparison with people ends!). What it *really* means is that you need to *bind* or wrap the ends of the rope.

◎ **Materials:**

• Cotton rope
• Sharp scissors or knife (use only with adult help)
• 2 feet (60 cm) of strong string, dental floss, twine, or fishing line

◎ **Description:** There are all kinds of whipping knots — a wrapped knot made from cord, monofilament, or fine string.

◎ **Uses:** To keep the end of a rope from unraveling, to mend a broken fishing pole, or to make a fancy finish on the end of a cord or stick.

HoW To Tie iT

❶ Cut and loop.

Cut off any frayed ends of the rope. Form a loop in the string and place it at the end of the rope, with one end of the string pointing in the same direction as the rope end and the other pointing down the rope.

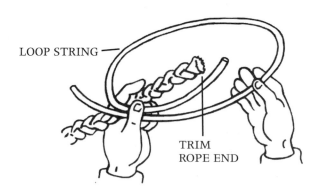

LOOP STRING

TRIM ROPE END

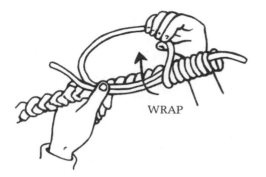

WRAP

❷ Wrap.

Tightly wrap (or "whip") the string around the rope, starting near the tip of the rope. Wrap back until the whipping is at least as long as the rope is wide.

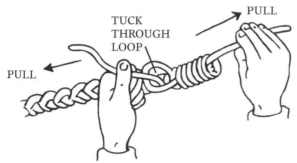

PULL

TUCK
THROUGH
LOOP

PULL

❸ Tuck.

Tuck the string end through the remaining loop. Pull the free ends of the string, dragging the loop under the middle of the whipping.

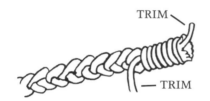

TRIM

— TRIM

❹ Trim.

Cut off the excess string at both ends of the whipping.

❺ Repeat.

Whip the other end of the rope the same way.

Fuse It!

Whipping works great on natural fibers, like cotton rope, but for synthetic (man-made) ropes (made of plastic, nylon, or any of the "new" fibers like Kevlar), *fusing* the ends of the rope by heating is better (and much easier).

Cut away any frayed ends of the rope. Then, *with adult supervision,* hold one end above a lighted candle or match to melt the very end (don't touch the melted rope end until it cools — it will be very hot and sticky!). Repeat with the other end, and let the rope cool.

Never try to fuse ropes made of natural fibers. They won't melt, they'll burn!

NYLON
ROPE

MELT
END

FUSED
END

CUT AWAY
FRAYED END

CANDLE

Constrictor Knot

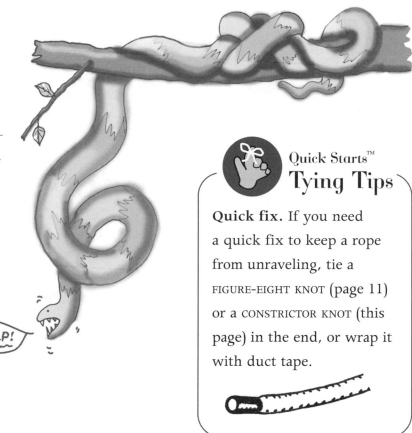

◎ Description: This knot has great gripping power — just like the snake that has the same name! You can trim the ends close to the knot and it'll still hold fast. It's actually a type of hitch — similar to a CLOVE HITCH (pages 46 to 47), but with an extra tuck. It's so useful as a binding knot, though, I've placed it here.

◎ Uses: For tying small bundles of loose material or for closing the necks of bags. Once called a WHIP KNOT, it can also be used as a temporary knot to keep the end of a cut rope from fraying.

HELP!

✂ Quick Starts™ Tying Tips

Quick fix. If you need a quick fix to keep a rope from unraveling, tie a FIGURE-EIGHT KNOT (page 11) or a CONSTRICTOR KNOT (this page) in the end, or wrap it with duct tape.

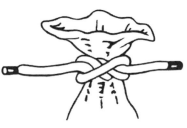

HOW TO TIE IT

❶ Wrap.
Take a full turn around the sack, crossing over the standing part of the rope.

❷ Wrap again.
Go around the sack again.

❸ Tuck.
Slip the working end over the standing part and under the first crossing.

❹ Tighten.
Pull tight.

WRAP

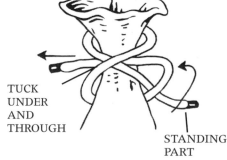

WRAP AGAIN

TUCK UNDER AND THROUGH

STANDING PART

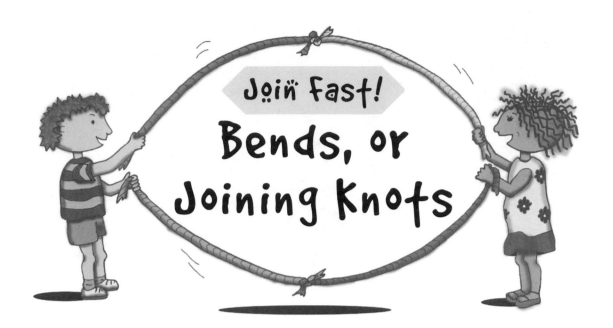

Join Fast!
Bends, or Joining Knots

A bend is the knot you need when you want to join two ropes together to temporarily form a longer rope — to make a gigantic jump rope or a longer towline, for instance. For a knot to be used as a bend, it must hold, even when jerked around or pulled from either end. The ropes joined should be sturdy, of the same *diameter* (thickness), and made of similar rope material. (The SHEET BEND, pages 14 to 15, is an exception: It is secure even when made of ropes of slightly different sizes.)

In a fix where you need a longer line in a hurry? Try a bend!

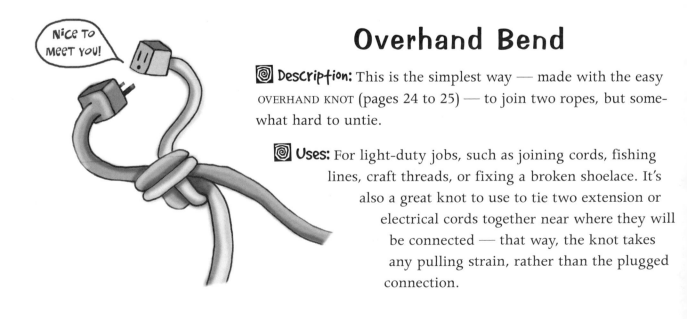

NICE TO MEET YOU!

Overhand Bend

◎ **Description:** This is the simplest way — made with the easy OVERHAND KNOT (pages 24 to 25) — to join two ropes, but somewhat hard to untie.

◎ **Uses:** For light-duty jobs, such as joining cords, fishing lines, craft threads, or fixing a broken shoelace. It's also a great knot to use to tie two extension or electrical cords together near where they will be connected — that way, the knot takes any pulling strain, rather than the plugged connection.

❶ Position.

Place the two ropes side by side, with the ends going the same way.

❷ Tie.

Make an OVERHAND KNOT (pages 24 to 25).

❸ Tighten.

Pull both ends snug.

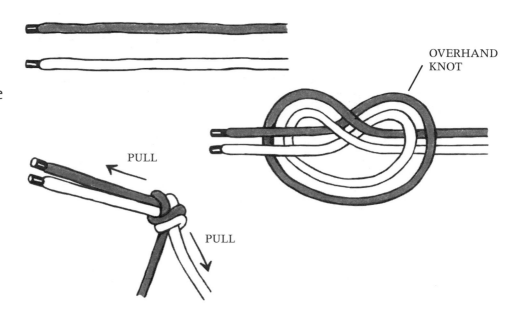

OVERHAND KNOT

PULL

PULL

Fisherman's Knot

BEADS

UMASS

◎ **Description:** This regular standby of fishermen and many other outdoor enthusiasts is just two OVERHAND KNOTS, each tied around the other rope. It makes a compact knot with streamlined ends, and is one of the easiest ways to join two lines together. It can be difficult to untie after being put under strain.

◎ **Uses:** Joining fishing lines, monofilament used for jewelry-making, weaver's yarn, thread, and other "small stuff." The bulkier and more secure doubled version is called the GRAPEVINE KNOT (see page 37).

HOW TO TIE IT

❶ Position.

Lay the ropes side by side, going in opposite directions.

❷ Tie.

Tie an OVERHAND KNOT (pages 24 to 25) as shown around the rope in one end.

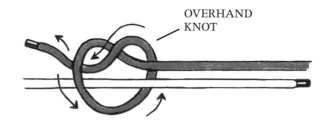

OVERHAND KNOT

❸ Tie again.

Tie a duplicate OVERHAND KNOT in the other rope, but going in the opposite direction and upside down. (If you turn the illustration upside-down, you'll see it's tied the same way as the other OVERHAND KNOT.) This is very important!

SECOND
OVERHAND
KNOT

❹ Tighten.

Tighten the two knots separately, then pull on the standing parts of both ropes so the knots slide together.

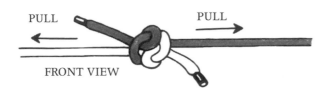

PULL

PULL

FRONT VIEW

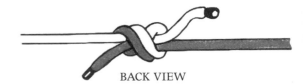

BACK VIEW

Quick Starts™
Tying Tips

Fast check. After the FISHERMAN'S KNOT is made, one end should lie *above* the knot and one end *below*. If you have trouble tying the second OVERHAND KNOT to match the first one (but upside down), turn your ropes so that you are tying it right-side up.

Knot Notes

Name game? Knot names are not always what they seem. The FISHERMAN'S KNOT, for instance, is used as a bend, but what is often called the FISHERMAN'S BEND (page 49) is actually a hitch!

Some knots also have several names, depending on how they are used, who discovered them, or the way they are tied. The RING HITCH (page 53) is also known as a LARK'S HEAD, and another name for a SHEET BEND (pages 14 to 15) is the WEAVER'S KNOT. And the CARRICK BEND (page 38) is known as the COWBOY KNOT to the cowhand and the WARP KNOT to the sailor. What should you call these multi-name knots? Use the name that's meaningful to *you*!

• **Grapevine, or double fisherman's knot.** A climbing favorite, the DOUBLE FISHER-MAN'S KNOT makes a bulky but secure knot, prized for joining two ropes. It is tied like the single FISHERMAN'S KNOT, except that you make *two wraps* for each identical OVERHAND KNOT as shown, and then tuck the end through *both* wraps.

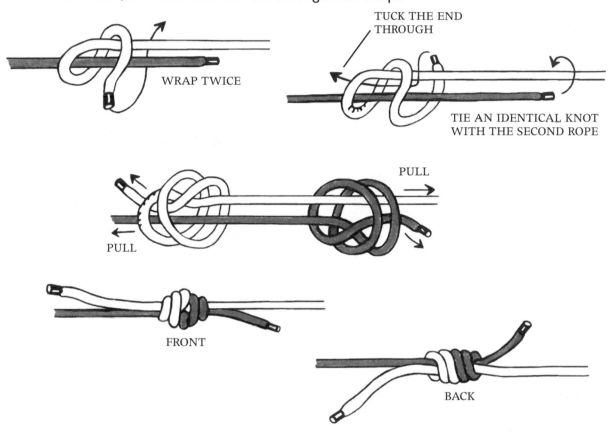

WRAP TWICE

TUCK THE END
THROUGH

TIE AN IDENTICAL KNOT
WITH THE SECOND ROPE

PULL

PULL

FRONT

BACK

• **Back it up.** Half of a DOUBLE FISHERMAN'S KNOT or GRAPEVINE KNOT is the best choice for using as a safety knot to keep a rope from slipping through another knot. Snug the half DOUBLE FISHERMAN'S KNOT right up to the edge of your main knot.

MAKE HALF OF A DOUBLE
FISHERMAN'S KNOT

SNUG UP NEXT
TO MAIN KNOT

Carrick Bend

BACK IN MY DAY . . .

⊚ **Description:** This bend has been in use for a thousand years! Though it looks tricky to do, it is actually very easy to tie — you just weave one rope over and under the other. It's a good way to join ropes that are the same size but made of different types of material. This knot can be difficult to untie if wet or after it's been under a lot of strain.

⊚ **Uses:** Good for joining cables and other larger ropes (such as for towing), as well as smaller ropes.

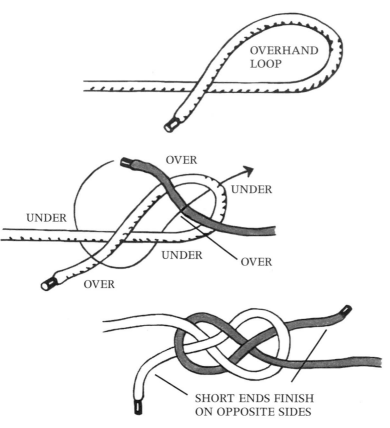

OVERHAND LOOP

OVER
UNDER
UNDER
UNDER
OVER
OVER
OVER

SHORT ENDS FINISH ON OPPOSITE SIDES

PULL
PULL

❶ **Loop.**
Make an overhand loop in one rope.

❷ **Weave.**
This is the fun part! Just weave the other rope over and under, over and under, and over and under, as shown.

❸ **Tighten.**
Pull on the standing parts of the ropes to tighten. The knot will "capsize" into a different shape.

Quick Starts™
Tying Tips

Short check. Before you pull the knot tight, make sure the short ends are on opposite sides of the knot.

40 KNOTS TO KNOW

Hunter's Bend

◎ **Description:** This is an especially good knot — discovered in the past sixty years — for joining nylon, polypropylene, or other slippery ropes. The double lock makes it grip well and stay stable, yet (unlike the CARRICK BEND on page 38) it can be loosened easily and untied by "breaking" the back.

◎ **Uses:** Good for ropes that will take a lot of strain, such as towropes, mooring lines, and dock lines.

HOW TO TIE IT

❶ Tie.

Make a loose OVERHAND KNOT as shown. Pass the end of the other rope down through the loop.

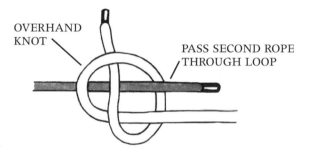

OVERHAND KNOT

PASS SECOND ROPE THROUGH LOOP

❷ Loop.

Loop the working end of the second rope under the standing part.

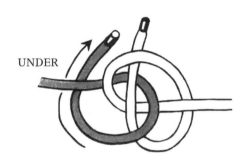

UNDER

❸ Tuck.

Tuck the working end of the second rope through the two loops as shown, passing next to the first working end. You've just made two interlocking knots!

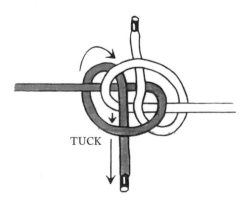

TUCK

❹ Tighten.

Pull the two working ends, then tighten the standing parts.

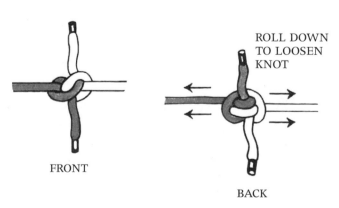

ROLL DOWN TO LOOSEN KNOT

FRONT

BACK

Knots that Make Loops

These knots join a rope to itself, making handy loops. Some knots make sliding, or "running," loops, like the one in a cowboy's lariat, a hunter's snare, or the fingerhold for your yo-yo string. Others, such as the trusty BOWLINE (page 12) and FIGURE-EIGHT LOOP (page 11), make secure nonslip loops you can use for rescues, camping, sailing, caving, and climbing — as well as for just tying stuff to the roof of your car!

Figure-Eight Loop

◎ **Description:** A secure nonslip all-purpose loop that can be tied (and untied) quickly and easily. It puts little stress on the rope when snugged up tight. Also called the GUIDE KNOT, or the FIGURE EIGHT ON A BIGHT.

◎ **Uses:** This variation of the FIGURE-EIGHT KNOT (page 11) is one of the most useful loops to know — it ranks right up there with the BOWLINE (page 12). It's great for climbing and rescue work because you don't need any free ends — the loop can be tied even if both ends of the rope are already tied to something else. For the same reason, it makes a super knot to know when you're lashing something to a car's roof rack (see pages 44 to 45).

HOW TO TIE IT

❶ **Make a bight.**
Make a long, narrow bight, doubling the rope.

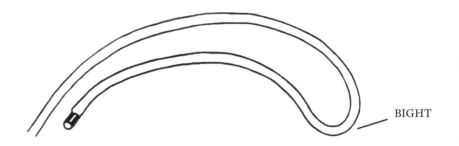

BIGHT

❷ Tie.

Tie a FIGURE-EIGHT KNOT (page 11) as shown using the doubled rope. Pull the loop through.

❸ Adjust and tighten.

Adjust the loop to the size you want and pull the unlooped part to tighten.

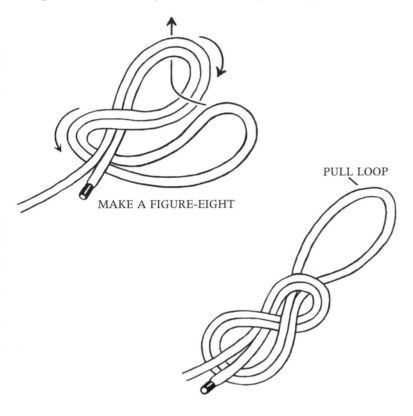

MAKE A FIGURE-EIGHT

PULL LOOP

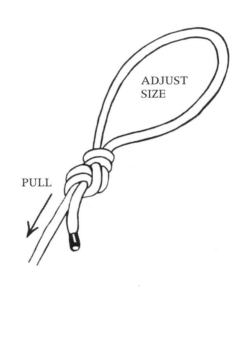

ADJUST SIZE

PULL

Quick Starts™
Tying Tips

Figure-eight retrace. This "rethreaded" way is used when you're tying the knot into something else. Make a loose single FIGURE-EIGHT KNOT, leaving plenty of loose rope at the end for the loop, and then weave that end back through the "eight," passing over and under the rope the same way.

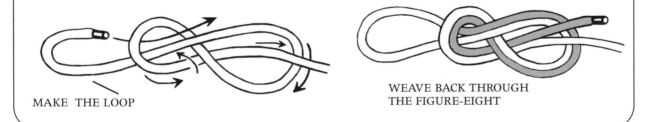

MAKE THE LOOP

WEAVE BACK THROUGH THE FIGURE-EIGHT

Alpine Butterfly

🌀 **Description:** This knot, also known as the BUTTERFLY KNOT, does the trick if you need a secure loop in the middle of a rope and you can't use the ends, though it's a little trickier to tie than the FIGURE-EIGHT LOOP (pages 40 to 41). The good thing about the ALPINE BUTTERFLY is that it keeps the main rope running in a straight line. It can be pulled from any direction.

🌀 **Uses:** Sometimes used for climbing, but also handy for tying gear down, because it doesn't slip. You could also use it as a quick handhold in a rope.

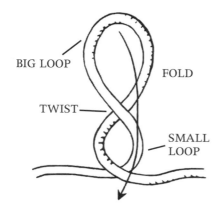

BIG LOOP

FOLD

TWIST

SMALL LOOP

How To Tie iT

❶ Loop.
Twist the standing part of the rope to make two loops, one big and one small. Then fold the big (outer) loop over the smaller one.

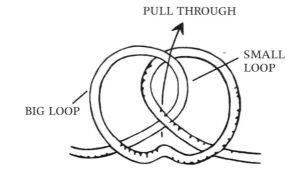

PULL THROUGH

SMALL LOOP

BIG LOOP

❷ Pull through.
Bring the big loop through the small loop.

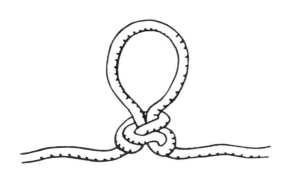

❸ Adjust and tighten.
Work the loop to the size you need, then tighten.

Slipknot

◎ **Description:** An OVERHAND KNOT (pages 24 to 25) tightened around the standing part of the line, this knot (also called a RUNNING KNOT) makes a simple sliding loop that tightens when pulled, such as for the fingerhold of your yo-yo string.

◎ **Uses:** This "running" loop can be used as a cowboy's lasso or around an object (such as a post). It's sometimes used for tying packages or tying items to a luggage rack, too.

HOW TO TIE IT

❶ Loop.

Make a loop as shown.

❷ Pull.

Pull the standing part of the rope through to make a loop. (What you actually have if you flip the knot is an OVERHAND KNOT, pages 24 to 25, tied over the standing part as shown in step 2.)

❸ Tighten.

Snug up the knot to tighten.

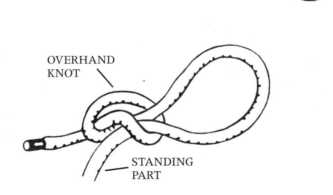

LOOP

PULL THROUGH

STANDING PART

OVERHAND KNOT

STANDING PART

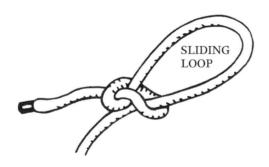

SLIDING LOOP

Knot Notes

Not for play! Though this knot can be very useful in the right situations, it can be deadly if used the wrong way. Another name for this knot is a SIMPLE NOOSE — *never, ever use it as a loop around a person!* Thank you.

Super-Simple Car-Rack Tie-Down

OK, let's put some of these loops (and some of the other knots you've learned so far) to use!

◎ **Description:** A system of loop knots and hitches that tightens easily, stays secure, and loosens without a tangle.

◎ **Uses:** Perfect for tying a Christmas tree to the top of a car; works well for tying on bulky, lightweight gear, too.

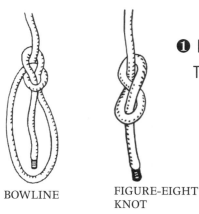

BOWLINE   FIGURE-EIGHT
KNOT

❶ Make a bowline.

Tie a BOWLINE (page 12) on one side of the rack. For extra security, add a stopper knot (such as a FIGURE-EIGHT KNOT, page 11) on the end.

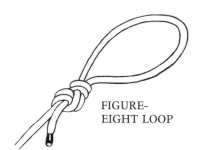

FIGURE-
EIGHT LOOP

❷ Tie a figure-eight loop.

Throw the rope over the gear, and tie a FIGURE-EIGHT LOOP (pages 40 to 41) in the rope about two feet (60 cm) from the other rack edge. Pass the working end of the rope around the rack, then back through the FIGURE-EIGHT LOOP to tighten the line.

❸ Tie two half hitches.

Pinching the tightened rope with one hand, so that it stays tight (very important!), tie TWO HALF HITCHES WITH A DRAW-LOOP (page 16) to secure the rope. First, tie one HALF HITCH around one rope. Then, tie the second HALF HITCH, leaving a draw-loop. To undo the tie-down, you just pull the draw-loop, and then pull the other hitch free, which will loosen the rope.

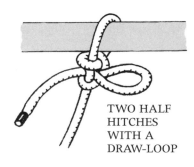

TWO HALF
HITCHES
WITH A
DRAW-LOOP

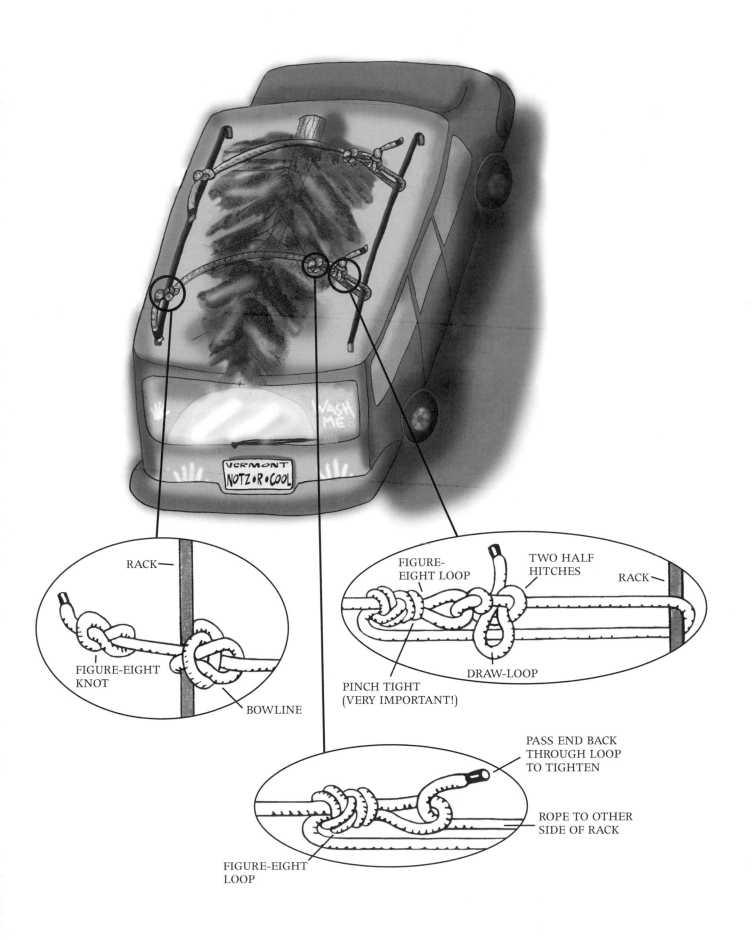

RACK —

FIGURE-EIGHT
KNOT

BOWLINE

FIGURE-
EIGHT LOOP

TWO HALF
HITCHES

RACK —

DRAW-LOOP

PINCH TIGHT
(VERY IMPORTANT!)

PASS END BACK
THROUGH LOOP
TO TIGHTEN

ROPE TO OTHER
SIDE OF RACK

FIGURE-EIGHT
LOOP

WASH
ME

VERMONT
NOTZ•R•COOL

Tying Ropes to objects

N eed to harness a pet to a post, secure a boat to a dock ring, hook up the clothesline, pitch a makeshift tent, or just hang stuff off your bunk bed? Hitches are the answer. These handy knots are used to tie ropes to or around fixed objects, such as a post, rail, ring, or peg. The rubbing force, or *friction* of the different wraps of the rope around itself or the object holds the hitch in place. Some, like the CLOVE HITCH (this page), are tied directly onto the object; others, such as the TAUT-LINE HITCH (page 50) and TWO HALF HITCHES (page 16) are looped around the object and then tied back to the rope itself. However you tie them, these knots do a lot of hard work!

Clove Hitch

◎ **Description:** If I added another hitch to the Fab Five (pages 10 to 18), this would be it. The clove in this knot's name comes from the word *cleave,* meaning "to hold fast." And, used correctly, that's just what the CLOVE HITCH does. It's easy to tie (and untie), and it won't jam under lots of strain.

◎ **Uses:** Use it when you'll have a steady pull *perpendicular* (at a right angle) to the knot — to hang something from a tree limb or railing, for instance. For extra security, the CLOVE HITCH is often used with other knots, such as TWO HALF HITCHES (page 48). The CLOVE HITCH is also the knot you use to start most lashings (pages 55 to 60).

How To Tie it

❶ Turn, cross, turn.

Wrap the end of the rope over and under the pole, then cross over this first turn and wrap it over and under again.

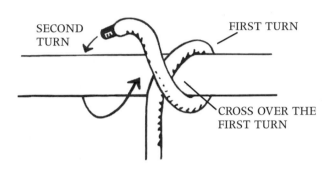

SECOND TURN

FIRST TURN

CROSS OVER THE FIRST TURN

❷ Tuck and tighten.

Tuck the end through the second turn and pull tight.

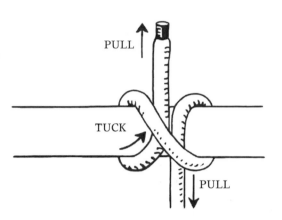

PULL

TUCK

PULL

Quick Starts™
Tying Tips

Tie it another way. Make an overhand loop near the end of the rope. Then make an underhand loop. Lay the underhand loop on top of the overhand loop. Place the two loops over the end of the post.

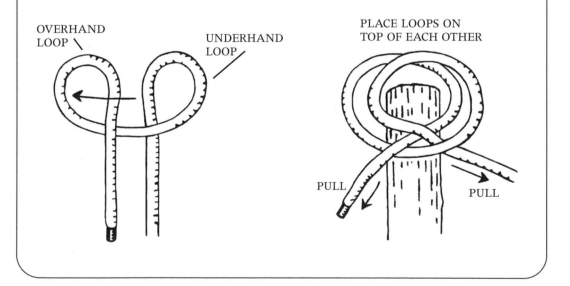

OVERHAND LOOP

UNDERHAND LOOP

PLACE LOOPS ON TOP OF EACH OTHER

PULL

PULL

• **Clove hitch with two half hitches.** If the pull on the rope isn't constant, the CLOVE HITCH may slip and come untied. Adding another favorite all-purpose hitch, TWO HALF HITCHES (page 16), makes the knot a lot more secure, yet still easy to work with. This variation is great for tying up a boat, and it makes a sturdy knot for a tire swing or pet tether, too.

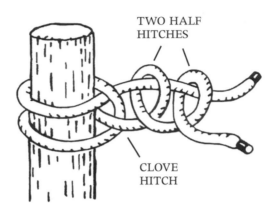

TWO HALF
HITCHES

CLOVE
HITCH

• **Slipped clove hitch.** For quick release, leave a draw-loop in the end of the rope when you poke the end through. To untie, you just pull on the free end, and the loop will slip open.

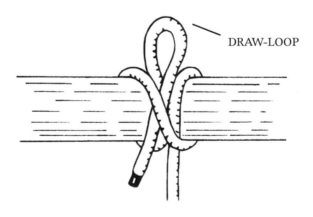

DRAW-LOOP

Fisherman's Bend

◎ **Description:** This variation of TWO HALF HITCHES (page 16) is good for slippery lines and synthetic ropes. It's one of the most secure hitches around.

◎ **Uses:** Traditionally the FISHERMAN'S BEND is used for mooring lines and dock lines, or tying to an anchor (it's also known as the ANCHOR BEND), but you could also use it for tying a rope to a ring, a rail, a tire, or other object.

HOW TO TIE IT

❶ Turn twice, then hitch.
Pass the end of the rope through the ring or around the rail two (or even three) times. Then pass the rope *through the turns* to form the first HALF HITCH.

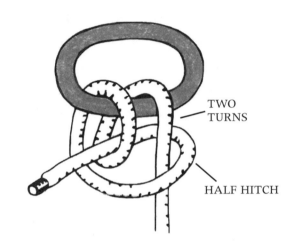

TWO TURNS

HALF HITCH

❷ Hitch, then tighten.
Make a second HALF HITCH around the standing part, just as you would for TWO HALF HITCHES (page 16, step 2). Snug the knot up tight by pulling on the standing part and the working end and pushing the hitches together.

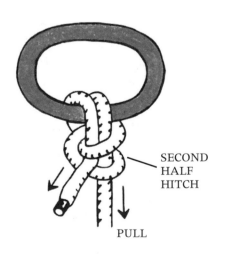

SECOND HALF HITCH

PULL

Taut-Line Hitch

Once you've mastered this knot, you'll find yourself using it all the time!

◎ **Description:** The TAUT-LINE HITCH forms an adjustable loop around an object, and the rope is then tied back onto itself. It slips only in one direction and grips where you want it to, keeping a line *taut,* or tight. You can adjust the tension on the rope by pushing the knot up or down, and — *ta-da!* — it stays in place. Handy? You bet!

◎ **Uses:** Ideal for the guylines of a tent or dining fly, or to keep a clothesline from flopping to the ground.

HOW TO TIE IT

❶ Loop, hitch, and turn.
Pass the working end of the rope around the object you're tying it to and then around the standing part of the rope, making a HALF HITCH. Then take another turn around the rope as shown.

❷ Pass and hitch.
Pass the rope across the knot and tie another HALF HITCH, farther up the standing part of the rope.

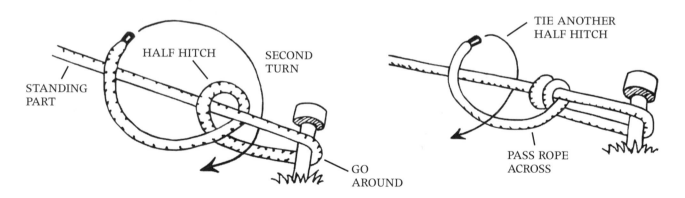

❸ Tighten.
Snug up the knot and slide the hitch to adjust the tension.

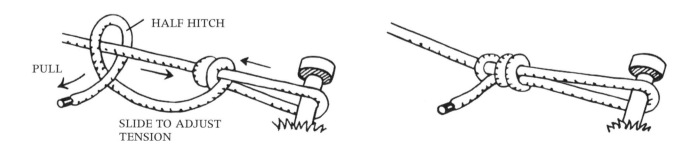

Timber Hitch

◎ **Description:** Here's a handy hauling hitch that's incredibly easy to tie and simple to undo. This is *not* a knot you can depend on for security, though. The TIMBER HITCH works best when it's tied around a rough, rounded surface (no wonder it's good for logs!) and the rope will have a slight, constant tug from one direction.

◎ **Uses:** Good for dragging awkward objects, logs, brush, or garden debris. It's also used to start a DIAGONAL LASHING (page 60).

HOW TO TiE iT

❶ Wrap and tuck.
Pass the end of the rope around the log or object and tuck it around the standing part of the rope, making a HALF HITCH (page 16, step 1).

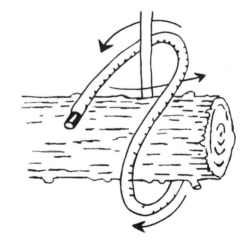

❷ Turn, turn, turn.
Wrap the end of the rope around itself three or more times.

❸ Tighten.
Pull ends to tighten.

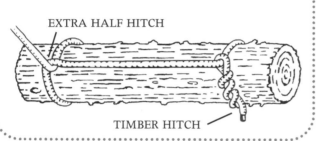

More Knots to Know

The Killick hitch. For hauling logs or bigger bundles of odd shapes, tie the TIMBER HITCH, and add an extra HALF HITCH near the front end to guide it along.

EXTRA HALF HITCH

TIMBER HITCH

Mooring Hitch

◎ **Description:** A hitch, also called the HITCHING TIE, made by making an underhand loop, a bight in the standing part, and a draw-loop. It can be tied quickly, holds securely under tension, and can be released with a tug on the working end.

◎ **Uses:** A favorite of canoeists and users of other small boats for temporarily mooring to a dock.

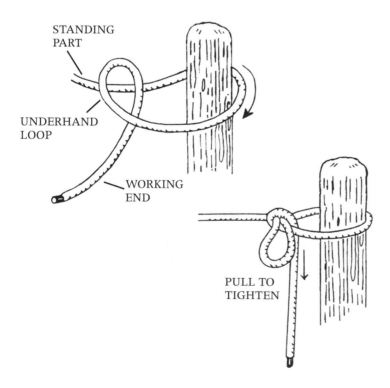

STANDING PART

UNDERHAND LOOP

WORKING END

PULL TO TIGHTEN

How To Tie It

❶ **Wrap and loop.**
Pass the end of the rope around the post or piling and then make an underhand loop in the working end.

❷ **Make a bight; pull it through.**
Make a bight in the *standing part* of the rope and pull it through the underhand loop. Pull the underhand loop tight.

❸ Make another bight; pull it through.

Make a bight in the *working end* of the rope and pull it through the loop you just made in the standing part. Pull on the standing part to tighten.

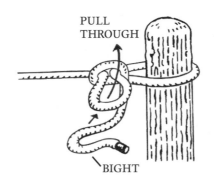

PULL THROUGH

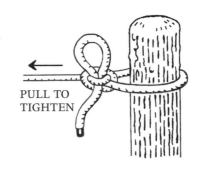

PULL TO TIGHTEN

BIGHT

Ring Hitch

 Description: This lightweight hitch, also known as the COW HITCH or LARK'S HEAD, is so simple you can tie it with a rubber band, though it also works with unlooped cord or rope.

Uses: Use it to hang or suspend lightweight objects, such as a stopwatch from your belt loop (I use it to carry my ski pass on a chain). Or, use it as a temporary animal tether.

HOW TO TIE IT

Tuck and tighten.

Pass the bight through the fastening ring. Then pass the loop over the object. Pull snug.

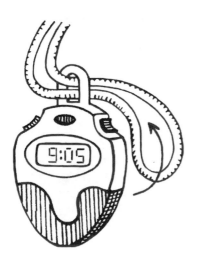

More Knots to Know

Lark's head or cow hitch. It's the same knot, just tied with a loose end.

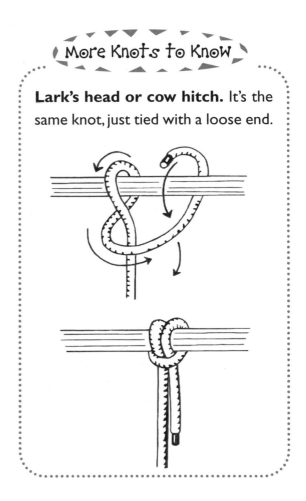

Cleat Hitch

◎ **Description:** A handy hitch that holds a rope to a cleat.

◎ **Uses:** It's especially good to know when you're securing a line on a boat or to a dock, but it's equally useful for snugging up a hoisted blind or Roman shade, or for fastening the halyard of a flag.

HOW TO TIE IT

❶ Turn.

Make one complete turn of the rope around the cleat.

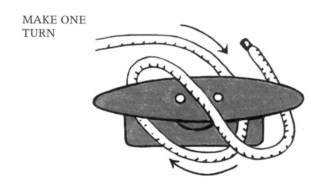

MAKE ONE TURN

❷ Tie and tuck.

Make a continuous figure eight under the "arms" of the cleat and across the top. Finish by tucking the rope under the last crossover, so the rope lies flat.

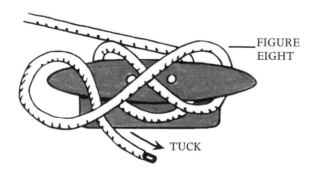

FIGURE EIGHT

TUCK

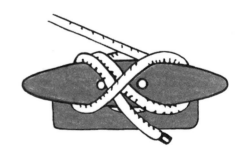

Lash It Together!

Building with Knots

OK, ready to put your knots to use? Lashings are special bindings that use hitches and turns to tie wood, stakes, or poles together. This is where you can really have some fun with your knot know-how! These practical bindings are just what you need to set up a bean tepee in your garden, construct a handy rack for your campsite, or build a table from sticks. You can use them for simple tasks, such as extending a flagpole; for emergencies (making a rescue stretcher or temporary shelter); or just for the fun of constructing a cool fort or a catapult.

Quick Starts™
Tying Tips

• **Small-world fun.** For starters, make model-sized structures using sticks and string. Build a footbridge or a 2' (60 cm) signal tower for a train set; beds or tables for a dollhouse; furniture (or even a tiny raft!) for Playmobil or Lego sets; or a railing for hitching up your model horses. You'll use all the same knots and turns that you'd use for full-sized structures!

• **How much rope?** For full-scale lashings, figure on about a yard (1 m) of rope for every inch (2.5 cm) of wood you'll be lashing together. For instance, if you'll be tying together two limbs that are 4" (10 cm) and 3" (7.5 cm) thick, you'll need about 7 yards (7 m) of rope.

Round Lashing

◎ **Description:** A simple system of one knot and a series of wraps to bind together two poles to make a longer pole.

◎ **Uses:** To make a flagpole or other long pole from two smaller poles.

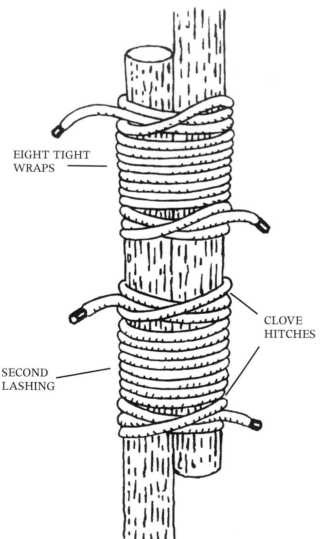

EIGHT TIGHT WRAPS

SECOND LASHING

CLOVE HITCHES

HOW TO TIE IT

❶ Hitch.

Place poles side by side. Tie a CLOVE HITCH (pages 46 to 47) around them.

❷ Wrap.

Make about eight very tight wraps around both poles.

❸ Finish.

Tie another CLOVE HITCH around the two poles.

❹ Repeat.

Make a second ROUND LASHING farther along the poles to keep them from twisting loose.

Shear Lashing

◉ **Description:** A series of knots and wraps to bind together two side-by-side poles of about the same height.

◉ **Uses:** To make an A-frame, for building bridges, tent frames, and other simple structures.

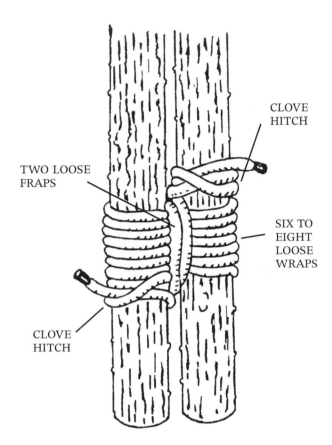

TWO LOOSE FRAPS

CLOVE HITCH

CLOVE HITCH

SIX TO EIGHT LOOSE WRAPS

HOW TO TIE IT

❶ Hitch.
Place the poles side by side. Tie a CLOVE HITCH (pages 46 to 47) around one of the poles.

❷ Wrap.
Make six to eight loose wraps around both poles, laying the wraps neatly side by side.

❸ Frap and finish.
Wind two loose fraps (see below) around the wraps *between the poles.* Tie a CLOVE HITCH around the other pole.

 Quick Starts™
Tying Tips

I'd like a frap. This is a *frap* (a knot wrap), not a *frappe* (a milkshake). *Frapping* turns are used to draw the rope wraps together to make the lashing tight.

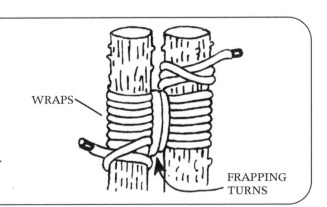

WRAPS

FRAPPING TURNS

Tripod Lashing

◎ **Description:** A SHEAR LASHING (page 57) with an extra pole, so the poles can be raised into a *tripod* — a three-legged stand or support.

◎ **Uses:** To make a bean tepee, a cooking tripod, or any other structure with three legs.

HOW TO TIE IT

❶ Hitch.

Place the poles side by side as shown. Tie a CLOVE HITCH (pages 46 to 47) around one outside pole.

❷ Wrap.

Make five to seven loose wraps around all three poles, laying the wraps neatly side by side.

❸ Frap.

Wind two loose fraps (page 57) on both sides of the center pole.

❹ Finish.

Tie a CLOVE HITCH around the center pole. Spread the poles into a tripod.

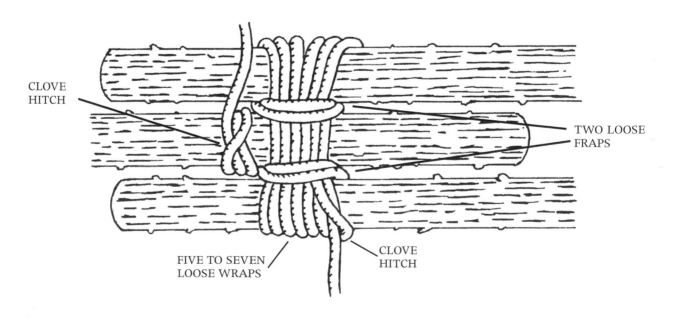

CLOVE
HITCH

TWO LOOSE
FRAPS

FIVE TO SEVEN
LOOSE WRAPS

CLOVE
HITCH

40 KNOTS TO KNOW

Square Lashing

🌀 **Description:** A series of knots and wraps to bind together two poles that are at right angles (*square* with one another).

🌀 **Uses:** To build a rack for hanging towels or wet clothes, to make crosspieces on a trestle or tower, or to make a makeshift bed or stretcher.

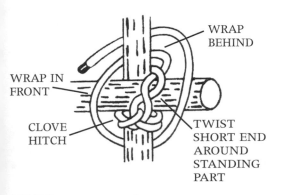

WRAP IN FRONT

WRAP BEHIND

CLOVE HITCH

TWIST SHORT END AROUND STANDING PART

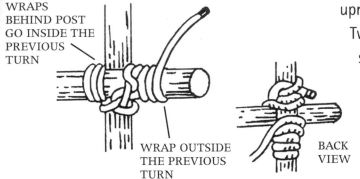

WRAPS BEHIND POST GO INSIDE THE PREVIOUS TURN

WRAP OUTSIDE THE PREVIOUS TURN

BACK VIEW

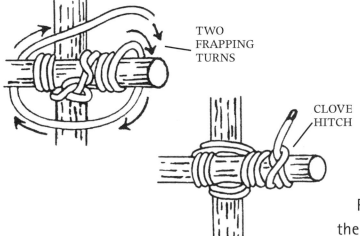

TWO FRAPPING TURNS

CLOVE HITCH

HOW TO TiE iT

❶ Hitch and wrap.

Place the poles at right angles *(square)* to one another. Tie a CLOVE HITCH (pages 46 to 47) around the upright pole, just below where the pieces cross. Twist the short end of the rope around the standing part to hold it in place. With the other end of the rope, make one wrap around both poles as shown, going *behind* the upright piece and *over* the front of the crosspiece.

❷ Wrap again.

Make two more tight wraps around both poles. Lay each new wrap on the *outside* of the previous turn of the crosspiece and on the *inside* of the previous turn on the upright pole.

❸ Frap.

Wind two fraps (page 57) *between the poles.*

❹ Finish.

Pull very tight. Tie a CLOVE HITCH around the crosspiece.

Diagonal Lashing

◎ **Description:** Similar to the SQUARE LASHING (page 59), but used when two poles are at any angle other than a right angle.

◎ **Uses:** To make any kind of structure that has wood attached at odd angles. Often used to attach crosspieces to sidepieces to make a tower or wall.

HOW To TIE iT

❶ Hitch.
Place the poles at the angle you want. Tie a TIMBER HITCH (page 51) around both poles; pull it snug.

❷ Wrap, and wrap again.
Make two to three tight wraps around both poles, *alongside* the TIMBER HITCH. Then make three *diagonal* wraps, as shown.

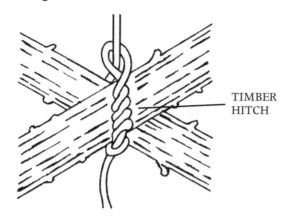

TIMBER HITCH

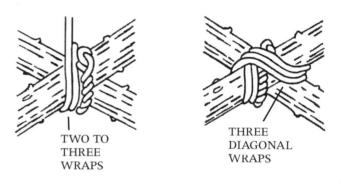

TWO TO THREE WRAPS

THREE DIAGONAL WRAPS

❸ Frap.
Wind two tight fraps (page 57) *between the poles.*

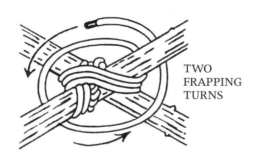

TWO FRAPPING TURNS

❹ Finish.
Tie a CLOVE HITCH (pages 46 to 47) around one pole.

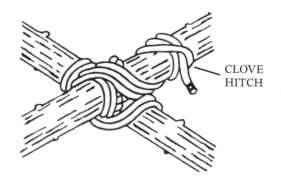

CLOVE HITCH

40 KNOTS TO KNOW

Resources

Recommended Knots

The following knots are required or recommended for each classification of Scouting, as well as for many merit badges:

 Boy Scouts

• *Cub Scout (Wolf)*
overhand bend (pages 34 to 35)
overhand knot (pages 24 to 25)
square knot (pages 17 to 18)

• *Cub Scout (Bear)*
bowline (pages 12 to 13)
coils (pages 19 to 21)
man overboard knot (overhand knot chain,
    page 25)
sheet bend (pages 14 to 15)
slipknot (page 43)
square knot (pages 17 to 18)
two half hitches (page 16)
whipping for rope ends
    (pages 31 to 32)

• *Cub Scout (Webelos)*
bowline (pages 12 to 13)
clove hitch (pages 46 to 47)
sheet bend (pages 14 to 15)
square knot (pages 17 to 18)
taut-line hitch (page 50)
two half hitches (page 16)

• *Tenderfoot Scout*
square knot (pages 17 to 18)
taut-line hitch (page 50)
two half hitches (page 16)
whip and fuse rope ends (pages 31 to 32)

• *First Class Scout*
bowline (pages 12 to 13)

clove hitch (pages 46 to 47)
diagonal lashing (page 60)
round lashing (page 56)
shear lashing (page 57)
sheet bend (pages 14 to 15)
square lashing (page 59)
timber hitch (page 51)
tripod lashing (page 58)

 Girl Scouts & Girl Guides

bowline (pages 12 to 13)
clove hitch (pages 46 to 47)
half hitch (page 16, step 1)
lark's head/ring hitch (page 53)
overhand knot (pages 24 to 25)
sheepshank (page 22)
sheet bend (pages 14 to 15)
square knot (pages 17 to 18)
taut-line hitch (page 50)
two half hitches (page 16)

For more information:
on Scouting programs, contact these sites:

• World Scouting
www.scout.org/

• World Association of Girl Guides and Girl Scouts
www.wagggsworld.org/

• U.S. Scouting
www.bsa.scouting.org/
www.girlscouts.org/

• Canadian Scouting
www.scouts.ca/
www.girlguides.ca/

Index

More Good Books from Williamson Publishing

Williamson books are available from your bookseller or directly from Williamson Publishing. Please see the next page for ordering information or to visit our website. Thank you.

Williamson's Kids Can!® Books...

Kids Can!® books for ages 6 to 14 are 128 to 176 pages, fully illustrated, trade paper, 11 x 8¹/₂, $12.95 US/$19.95 CAN.

Parents' Choice Recommended
THE KIDS' BOOK OF WEATHER FORECASTING
Build a Weather Station, "Read" the Sky & Make Predictions!
with meteorologist Mark Breen and Kathleen Friestad

American Bookseller Pick of the Lists
Parents' Choice Approved
SUMMER FUN!
60 Activities for a Kid-Perfect Summer
by Susan Williamson

Selection of Book-of-the-Month; Scholastic Book Clubs
KIDS COOK!
Fabulous Food for the Whole Family
by Sarah Williamson and Zachary Williamson

Parents' Choice Gold Award
Dr. Toy Best Vacation Product
THE KIDS' NATURE BOOK
365 Indoor/Outdoor Activities and Experiences
by Susan Milord

Parents' Choice Approved
Dr. Toy Best Vacation Product
KIDS GARDEN!
The Anytime, Anyplace Guide to Sowing & Growing Fun
by Avery Hart and Paul Mantell

Parents' Choice Approved
Parent's Guide Children's Media Award
BOREDOM BUSTERS!
The Curious Kids' Activity Book
by Avery Hart and Paul Mantell

The Kids' Guide to
MAKING SCRAPBOOKS & PHOTO ALBUMS!
How to Collect, Design, Assemble, Decorate
by Laura Check

Parents' Choice Recommended
KIDS' ART WORKS!
Creating with Color, Design, Texture & More
by Sandi Henry

Parents' Choice Gold Award
Benjamin Franklin Best Juvenile Nonfiction Award
KIDS MAKE MUSIC!
Clapping and Tapping from Bach to Rock
by Avery Hart and Paul Mantell

Parents' Choice Gold Award
American Bookseller Pick of the Lists
THE KIDS' MULTICULTURAL ART BOOK
Art & Craft Experiences from Around the World
by Alexandra M. Terzian

Benjamin Franklin Best Education/Teaching Gold Award
Parent's Guide Children's Media Award
HAND-PRINT ANIMAL ART
by Carolyn Carreiro
full color, $12.95

Parents' Choice Honor Award
THE KIDS' NATURAL HISTORY BOOK
Making Dinos, Fossils, Mammoths & More
by Judy Press

 # Williamson's Quick Starts for Kids!® Books

Quick Starts for Kids!® books for children, ages 8 and older, are each 64 pages, fully illustrated, trade paper, 8¹/₂ x 11, $8.95 US/$10.95 CAN.

Dr. Toy 100 Best Children's Products
Dr. Toy 10 Best Socially Responsible Products
MAKE YOUR OWN BIRDHOUSES & FEEDERS
by Robyn Haus

YO-YO!
Tips & Tricks from a Pro
by Ron Burgess

GARDEN FUN!
Indoors & Out; In Pots & Small Spots
by Vicky Congdon

Oppenheim Toy Portfolio Gold Award
DRAW YOUR OWN CARTOONS!
by Don Mayne

DRAWING HORSES
(that look *real!*)
by Don Mayne

Parents' Choice Approved
BAKE THE BEST-EVER COOKIES!
by Sarah A. Williamson

MAKE YOUR OWN FUN PICTURE FRAMES!
by Matt Phillips

MAKE YOUR OWN CHRISTMAS ORNAMENTS
by Ginger Johnson

BE A CLOWN!
Techniques from a Real Clown
by Ron Burgess

Really Cool
FELT CRAFTS
by Peg Blanchette and Terri Thibault

KIDS' EASY KNITTING PROJECTS
by Peg Blanchette

KIDS' EASY QUILTING PROJECTS
by Terri Thibault

MAKE YOUR OWN HAIRWEAR
Beaded Barrettes, Clips, Dangles & Headbands
by Diane Baker

American Bookseller Pick of the Lists
**MAKE YOUR OWN TEDDY BEARS &
BEAR CLOTHES**
by Sue Mahren

ALMOST-INSTANT SCRAPBOOKS
by Laura Check

KIDS' EASY BIKE CARE
Tune-Ups, Tools & Quick Fixes
by Stephen Cole

MAKE MAGIC!
50 Tricks to Mystify & Amaze
by Ron Burgess

Visit our Website!
www.williamsonbooks.com

To order Books:

We accept Visa and MasterCard (*please include the number and expiration date*). Toll-free phone orders with credit cards:

1-800-234-8791

Fax orders with credit cards:
1-800-304-7224

Or, send a check with your order to:

Williamson Publishing Company
P.O. Box 185
Charlotte, Vermont 05445

Catalog request: mail, phone, or e-mail

<info@williamsonbooks.com>

Please add $4.00 for postage for one book plus $1.00 for each additional book. Satisfaction is guaranteed or full refund without questions or quibbles.